This Is <u>NOT</u> That: How to Keep Demons from Coming at You

by Dr. Marlene Miles

https://marlenemilestheauthor.com/

ISBN: 978-1-960150-23-3

Dear Reader:

Thank you for acquiring and reading this book. May it spark the change that you've been looking for.

This Is <u>NOT</u> That

Freshwater

Freshwater Press

USA

Contents

The book you don't read
could be the book that tells your life,
or saves your life.
Read this book.

This Is How Much I Have to Tell Them

When someone emails or calls me to ask me about something deeply evil and deeply spiritual that they are going through, this book is how much I have to tell them to get them to even *begin* to think about their problem, to understand it and begin to solve it by Jesus Christ and the power of His Blood, His Name, and by the power of His Holy Spirit.

I will not be able to talk to any one person this long in one conversation and I will not write an email that is this long to *begin* to explain to a person what their problem might be, especially when, except by the Holy Spirit, will I **know** what they are doing, have done or have in their ancestry to cause what is happening to them.

Sometimes people don't tell you the whole truth even when the Holy Spirit is telling you that they are involved in thus or so. All people are not deceitful, some don't think there is anything at all wrong with the way they are conducting their lives and their spirituality, even though it might be the worst –, completely demonic. Some are oppressed of evil spirits that will either not let them answer truthfully but may also be manifesting and answering *for* the human who is asking you for help.

Many may be, by family tradition, convenience, or by the advice of friends unable, or unwilling to see anything wrong with the things they do or don't do, spiritually speaking.

A lot of the time I see that people have tried to mix "religions." Nope can't do that. God hates blends. He even told the Israelites to not mix wool and linen fabric together. Plus, mixing another "religion" in with Christianity is still idolatry. The Israelites got into the most trouble, repeatedly, and cyclically by worshipping strange *gods*--, idolatry. (See the Book of Judges.)

So here is the book that will get a lot of people to the **starting point** of understanding what, why, where things may have gone wrong, spiritually.

I have to write this down because how can I call a person a liar? Therefore, the Holy Spirit will have to convict the reader of Truth.

How can I tell them that the thing that they are practicing thinking it is a *religion* is not a religion at all? How can I tell someone who may be deceived that their spiritual practices are fully demonic? Or, partially demonic? Not of God at all? I can, however, tell them to read this book and let the truth speak for itself.

First, if you are serious about Christianity and Jesus Christ, get saved. Don't tell me you're already saved. If you are saved, you will get up and accept Jesus Christ again every morning of your life and rededicate yourself to Christ every single day over and over because it's who you are and what you do. There is nothing, no negative spiritual influences or oppression impeding you from that.

Receive the Holy Spirit. If someone can minister the Holy Spirit to you, great. If not just pray and ask God. I received the Holy Spirit alone in my house one day praying with a TV minister. Knocked me down. It was awesome!

Commit to Jesus Christ and practice the Disciplines of the Faith.

Renounce idolatry and idol religions, cults. Repent. There is a lot of work to do. We'll talk more about this at the end of the book, but first let's make sure we are really practicing Christianity by learning what is NOT serving Christ, what is NOT Christian behavior or acts.

Know Something About It

If someone told you that you were a boy and you knew nothing about boys, or being a boy, wouldn't you feel frustrated or unsure? Wouldn't you want to find out about boys?

If you were pregnant and you were having a boy, wouldn't you want to know at least something, if not *everything* about boys? I know a man who was stressing because he had a daughter, but he and his wife were pregnant with a boy. His stress was that he didn't think he'd know what to do with a boy, how to dress a boy, how to raise a boy. Huh? He's a male, himself. *Anyhoo…*

Well, you are a spirit.

What do you know about *spirits*?

What do you know about spiritual things?

For parents, you have a spirit; your child or children are spirits. For parents to-be, your child/children will be spirits. What do you know of spirits or spiritual things? For all humans in the Earth: You **ARE** a spirit. What do you know of spirits or spiritual things?

Sadly, most of us don't know about spirits or spiritual things. Somehow and for some reason it has been dismissed as something we don't need to know anything about. Why?

You tell me.

Sadly, most people stop or want to know little else after they find out the gender of a baby that's coming into their family. What will he/she look like? What color hair, skin, eyes? That's about it. Why? Why do they care to know so little?

Since God breathes life into this baby, I'd want to know who this person is *to God*. Is this a pastor, teacher, prophet, apostle or evangelist? Is this a person of the 5-fold ministry and what is my *responsibility* to this baby?

Not knowing anything spiritual about a child is why parents don't train their children up in the way that they should go. And, it is why and how the world can get their hands on children, young adults, people in general and mold them into things that God never intended. Not knowing anything spiritual or being trained in or trained INCORRECTLY in spiritual things is how spiritual virtues, gifts, skills, and abilities are stolen from folk every day of the week.

Spiritual stuff? Oh, that's all or only for the pastor to know? Do you only let a chef prepare all your meals and you know nothing of food? The medical doctor? The dentist: Don't answer this, but do you never brush or floss your teeth because the dentist or hygienist will do it twice a year for you?

Okay so we realize we need to be realistic to be successful here in the Earth.

Do you know nothing of home repairs because they have *people* for that? Of course not, you mow the lawn, cook meals, change light bulbs and batteries. Right?

Man comes to Earth. He's a *spirit*, he has a soul, and he lives in a body, but he only cares about the body, the flesh. He only cares about the temporal thing, the thing that will last him the least amount of time – say 100 years or so. Maybe more by reason of strength and the Grace of God.

Years ago, a young man told me that his mother told him if you're not really smart then be sure to develop your body. I suppose she was saying, *Play to your strengths.* If a person's body is their strength, or their only strength, are we all body builders, then? No, that's not the case at all.

Some are more emotional than others and live their entire lives focusing on their emotions primarily. Emotions are an upgrade in that they influence the flesh, but sometimes the flesh can influence the soul. For example, if you are in pain you might be cranky.

A person could be captive to their emotions. They could be overwhelmed or run by their flesh or some combination of that. We've discussed in previous books that the spirit of a man should be running both the soul and the flesh, and the spirit of man should be governed by the Spirit of God.

(See **Upgrade: How to Get Out of Survival Mode** by this author.)

You Think You're Saved

You may think you're saved because your grandmother or other relative is/was saved or because you went to church as a child. Being churched is not the same as being saved. That's not how this works. Being saved is not inherited. You have to accept Jesus Christ as your Lord and Savior yourself and then work out your Salvation with fear and trembling.

Sinner's Prayer

Lord Jesus, this is my simple prayer to You. I know that I am a sinner and that I often fall short of the glory of God. No longer will I close the door when I hear You knocking. By faith, I gratefully receive Your gift of salvation. I'm ready to trust You as my Lord and Savior.

Thank You, Lord Jesus, for coming to Earth. I Believe You are the Son of God who died on the cross for my sins and rose from the dead on the third day. Thank You for Your forgiveness of sins and for giving me the gift of eternal life. I invite Jesus to come into my heart and be my Savior. In the Name of Jesus, Amen.

Prayer To Receive Holy Spirit

Heavenly Father, I come to You asking You, in Jesus's Name to fill me with Your Holy Spirit, to baptize me in His fire, and to clothe me in His power, in the Name of Jesus.

Amen.

A Prisoner

The easiest prisoner to maintain is one that doesn't even know he's been captured. Until it's too late--, if ever.

You'd be able to tell if your flesh was *captured*, right? Ropes, zip ties, prison bars?

How about your soul?

How about your spirit? Could you tell if your spirit had been captured or was under lockdown? Most, probably not. Therefore, we surmise then that most people ONLY know about their flesh. They use their five senses overtime to know about the status of their flesh and the flesh of others which they may be ogling at any time of the day or night.

More enlightened people may know something of the souls and *spirits* of others, as the freedom or captivity of a soul or spirit is ascertained by the Spirit. The Spirit of God is chiefly how this should be known.

Too many people think they have found a way to circumvent God and that's where the devil comes in and that's how souls and spirits end up captured and on lockdown. Read my book, **Souls in Captivity** for much more on this topic.

Anything God is offering mankind the devil tries to copy and then offers man a shortcut, such as blessings with no spiritual work, like bait in a mousetrap; the devil is treating mankind like varmints to be captured.

Please know that this baiting is **ALWAYS** a trick. **Also know that ANYTHING you get from the devil will cost you EVERYTHING--,** if not immediately, certainly over time. If not in your time, in your lifetime, in the time of your *children*. If not in their time, then in the time of your *children's* children... your grandchildren. The unsaved are considered to hate God. Their sins carry iniquity into the 10th to 14th generations of their bloodlines. That's a loooooonnnnngggg time.

But if you don't even know that you are captive, you will do nothing to free yourself, to save yourself, or reach out to JESUS for Salvation and deliverance.

Jesus said that deliverance is the children's bread. People of God, when we are captive we will be *fed* in the dream by evil, unknown, invisible, masquerading captors. When we are free we should be seeking the Bread of Life and the BREAD that is our deliverance and eating that ONLY. Get out your Bible and read the Word. Listen to the Word. Saturate in the Word and deliverance will either come by the washing of the water by the Word or if you need a deliverance minister the process will be more efficient.

The Rules

But you either know, swear or believe you haven't done anything to cause this evil that has befallen you. And you may not have done anything to cause it, but you are somebody's child, and you are also the child of somebody's child. You are the second generation of someone. You are the third generation of someone(s). You are the 4th generation of some people, even people who believe and say they love God.

Unfortunately, you may be the 10th to the 14th generation of people who do not love God. These are the reasons why *things* could be happening to you. Witchcraft may be in your bloodline; it may be in your blood, and you may not even know it. If your mother is a witch, even a blind witch, then you're a witch or warlock. If your father is/was a warlock, then you're a witch or warlock. By this designation demons have the right to come into your life even if you never sin a day in your life. This could be why things are happening to you: **evil foundation.**

Man ought to always repent. Sometimes sin is hidden to us. Yes, we can sin 24 hours a day, even in the sleep, in the dream, but also, we may do things by tradition or habit that might be sins and we don't know either that it's a sin, or that we did it. Job made offerings for his kids just in case they had sinned. Job tried to do right, and he got *tried* horrendously--, how much more for some who do not even TRY to live right before the Lord.

Unless you renounce and repent witchcraft down your ancestral line that witchcraft will stay in your blood. Most of the time a person whose parents don't know that they, themselves are witches or have never told their children that they practiced witchcraft (unrepented) will only know this when weird, evil, unexpected things happen in *their* lives. For example, a woman keeps attracting warlocks as suitors and husbands, or a man keeps marrying witches. It's in the blood.

That is not necessarily and always the case, though. Marrying a warlock for a husband or a witch for a wife may be a curse assigned to a person for other sins. Yes, it's complicated; that's why we have to work out our Salvation with fear and trembling.

Looking at what's going on in your world, you may become indignant and do nothing, either falling into denial or becoming angry that your life is not going according to your plans or desires. Perhaps you haven't done either. Thank goodness!

Perhaps you have done both, making things even worse. Could be that you don't even know what you did because you don't know what the rules (laws) are. The rules of any game, basketball, board game, chess, backgammon, video games... we are careful to find out what those rules are and those are *games*.

Your real life is <u>not</u> a game. It might be to the devil, but it shouldn't be to you. The results will not determine if you compete for the $10,000. cooking championship or get a big belt with a big buckle or a huge, shiny trophy, but it will determine life and death and your <u>Eternity</u>.

The most egregious thing is when people are so deceived that they end up reaching out to the entity that enslaved them to get relief or be set free. This tightens the snare, increases the bondage of their imprisonment, layers on the chains. It deepens the pit of captivity, reinforces the locks, the torment, the torture and the generational bondage.

I remember being so ignorant that just because I had a spiritual dream I thought that was good, never trying to find out WHAT did that dream mean and what should I do about it. In so doing, I accepted a lot of stuff that I should have prayed about immediately, I should have canceled, and I should have increased my prayer life and changed what I was doing in my natural life instead of thinking I was "deep" because I had a dream (or dreams) and at least recognized that they were *spiritual*.

Furthermore, I did not seek Christian and Biblical dream interpretation. No, I might pick up a book or go online and look up any random dream interpretation, until I read what I WANTED the dream to mean. Usually that interpretation celebrated ME. Warning: Please don't do this. At the dream stage things are way easier to stop, handle, and or fix. The dream stage is the spiritual stage. By the time it gets to you in the natural world it will be SO HARD to deal with--, IF you can ever get out of it.

This Is NOT That

We interrupt our regularly scheduled programming --, we now interrupt what we were doing or were going to do--, to bring you, **This Is NOT That** because it has become glaringly obvious that many people who _say_ they worship Jesus Christ and that they serve the Only Living God are confused.

They either don't know _who_ they are serving, **how** to serve Jesus, or they've layered so many mismatched things together, they are following family tradition or culture, or they just do whatever seems convenient on any given day. They seem not to know what sins are--, what is a sin. They don't know what idolatry is, what witchcraft is or when they have crossed the line out of Christianity into evil and _all evil_, which God not only judges but when you do this, God also takes His hands of protection off you and that is why you have demons and the like coming at you as soon as you close your eyes at night and sometimes in the daytime also.

Strange religions have been **conflated** with traditional Christianity to create some kind of a homemade, Frankenstein, personal, or mutt religion that is comfortable to the user. There is an entire landscape of people who are wandering from pillar to post doing what *feels* right to them. Even if they all agree on their individual or collective practices, if GOD doesn't agree, then it is **sin.**

God is long suffering and patient, but when a person sins and they don't repent, they open the door for evil into their lives. They are often inundated with spiritual stimuli that is tormenting them, damaging them, that they desperately do not understand but want to be rid of.

Allegedly many are seeing "visions" of angels and Jesus Christ coming to "rescue" them, while people who are sincerely serving the Only Living God are not having demons charging at them during the day and the night because there is not a flurry of dramatic and theatre-worthy apparitions bombarding them day and night. Jesus is **not** coming to their house, in person, every day--, it seems that Jesus is personally rescuing these people who are in idolatry.

What?

I am not the only one approached by such a person, usually in dramatic turmoil and they want prayers. They seek prayers. They ***need*** prayers. So, the prayers begin. More often than not it takes usually days and most often weeks to get to the core of the problem, to even to begin to pray the right prayers.

Christianity is not a smoothie where you throw in all the stuff you like and press, *Blend*.

In the search for the truth, we find out the demonics that the average, unsuspecting, **religion-blended** person has invited into their own life. We keep listening to learn that they have become overwhelmed and are searching, searching, searching and egging someone, anyone to please pray for them. They need someone, anyone to make the torment stop and take away the fear and it's torment.

The problem is, if you don't know what caused it, it will either not go away or go away for a little while, but as soon as you resume your same lifestyle that caused the torment, it will be right back again. Stronger than ever.

When the unclean spirit is gone out of a man, he walketh through dry places, seeking rest, and findeth none.

Then he saith, I will return into my house from whence I came out; and when he is come, he findeth it empty, swept, and garnished.

Then goeth he, and taketh with himself seven other spirits more wicked than himself, and they enter in and dwell there: and the last state of that man is worse than the first. Even so shall it be also unto this wicked generation. Matthew 12:43-45

Deliverance is the children's bread, that means deliverance is for saved people. An unsaved person can be delivered, as Legion in the Gadarenes, but most often the person who has actively blended all kinds of religions and practices together is not a candidate for deliverance. Yes, demons will obey the person ministering the deliverance, most of the time. But deliverance is subject to the person hosting the demons. If they have invited the demons and haven't stopped whatever caused them to be there, there will be no deliverance.

Further, the demons will return stronger after the deliverance minister goes home or the candidate leaves church if NOTHING has changed in their life, namely Salvation in Jesus Christ and the infilling of the Holy Spirit.

No One Believes Me

Another real problem is that no one believes them. It is hard for the average person, even a pastor to believe these theatre style demon oppressions and attacks if that pastor doesn't know anything about or believe in deliverance. That pastor will be dismissive of the person's problem or problems.

The symptoms of the need for deliverance may be hidden for a long time. The symptoms may be non-existent or so random--, and there is no guidebook to look up what your loved one may be telling you so you may not believe them.

Spiritual information that should have been passed on to your generations verbally, because all the people in your family are *spirits* was not passed into your generations. You know, the memo where you teach your children at all times-

-, no one in your family got that memo. Was it because your family became affluent and decided that only poor people believe in demons and stuff like that? Perhaps your family became educated in universities and decided that only **ignorant** people believe in *spirits* and all that jazz. So, someone in your family line either stopped teaching their children anything spiritual at all, or the children became wise in their generation and stopped *listening* to their parents because parents are just so old fashioned. Perhaps your family had "*arrived*" according to your standards.

Or someone in your family bloodline went to unscrupulous, ungodly means to get relief or success in life and they can't tell anyone because they'd be telling on themselves. Possibly the oaths they made along the way would cause them loss, death, or worse. (Which it will anyway, it's just that it will come quicker if they break an oath, especially a blood--or a death oath.) Maybe they won't tell because they are embarrassed.

If practicing witchcraft is a way of life for a family, they won't think there is anything wrong with it. They think that demons are nice spirits that will help them and that these nice spirits (spirit guides) are manageable, controllable --, but later they find out these *spirits this energy they think they have control over,* are demons that cannot be controlled or managed, especially when the come to a person's house/home/body to live bringing others so now they are many.

This is when the phone calls start, or a person may put on their nicest clothes and go to a church. But, if there is no power in the church, what next? People ask their family and friends, who know little or nothing about being a spirit.

Here's where they really get trapped, they go back to the place where their problem started to try to get a solution there. The problem is demons. The problem is witchcraft. The problem is hell. The problem is the devil. The problem is you, until you get saved and Spirit-Filled, resist the devil instead of calling on him, or worse, *repeatedly* calling on him and his minions.

What Is Sin?

You are responsible for knowing what sin is,-- what are the sins just as you are responsible to know what a crime is in the natural. Sin is a *spiritual crime*, so it's no different, although it is far worse. It is a grave decision or mistake to sin against the Most Holy God, or to fall into the hands of God when He is angry. The punishment for sin may be spiritual, soulish and/or natural. Most often it is all three. But it is death.

How so? Spiritual crimes are answered with spiritual judgments, and spiritual punishments.

From the spirit there is or will be an effect on the soul. The soul then affects the flesh. So, by the time you *feel* a manifestation in your flesh, minutes, hours, days, weeks, years, even decades or GENERATIONS later it could have been the result of a spiritual crime committed a long time ago. That sin could have been committed by your ancestors, but **you** feel it.

The children's teeth are set on edge from something the parents ate. The parents (ancestors) enjoyed something, let's say that something is sin, but the children are paying for it. Great-Grandpa was not spiritual and knew nothing of being a spirit --, he was only flesh-natured. So, he committed some sin that his flesh really enjoyed, and nothing happened **in his flesh** so he believed nothing will happen, that he got away with it. God is patient, but He will require an answer for unrepented sin. God may require a punishment for repented for sin, but the repentance is like an allocution where the punishment is far less because the sinner confessed, repented and begged Mercy of God. But Great-Grandpa didn't, so here comes the punishment into your generation, into your life.

Have you ever considered that you have probably had MORE than one ancestor that SINNED & didn't repent. Lord, help us all.

The fathers have eaten sour grapes, and the children's teeth are set on edge. (Eze 18:2b)

Ten Commandments

These are the Ten Commandments, but that's not all there is to Christianity. It is a good start, however.

- **You will have no other *gods* before me.**
- **You will not make idols.**
- **You will not take the name of the Eternal God in vain.**
- **Remember the Sabbath day to keep it holy.**
- **Honor your father and your mother.**
- **You will not kill.**
- **You shall not commit adultery.**
- **You will not steal.**
- **You shall not speak false testimony against your neighbor.**
- **You will not covet.**

Works of the flesh: Now the works of the flesh are evident: sexual immorality, impurity, sensuality, idolatry, sorcery, enmity, strife, jealousy, fits of anger, rivalries, dissensions, divisions, envy, drunkenness, orgies, and things like these.

Galatians 5:19-21 NLT

     The above verses list the works of the flesh. Add those flesh works to the Ten Commandments to get a better grasp on what sins are. The following will be an outline of other and related sins to bring clarity to what a person may be doing wrong, or not doing at all that is bringing demonic oppression into their life. Read on, but know this is just a start.

Atheism

An atheist does not believe that God is--, the God exists. He can also deny that there is rain but when he goes outside, he will get wet. People who don't know you and don't know me can swear (don't swear) that we do not exist, but we do. Just because you are ignorant of a person, or a thing does not take it out of existence.

By denying that there is God the atheist falls directly into the trap that the devil has set which states that he, the devil, does not exist. It is the greatest lie, that has ever been told, and believed.

By closing his eyes to truth, the atheist is as the little child who also closes his eyes and believes that no one can see him while his eyes are closed. The atheist somehow believes that not believing in a thing will protect him from that thing. It won't.

If you are one such person, anything could come into your life.

Agnosticism

An agnostic thinks he's more clever than the atheist and believes that whether there is God or that there is God is *unknowable*. In so stating, he is letting everyone know that *he* is unsaved and that he does not have the Holy Spirit or any of the seven Spirits of God. The seven Spirits that are around the Throne of God: the Spirit of the Lord, the Spirits of Wisdom, understanding, counsel, might, knowledge and of fear of the LORD.

God reveals Himself to people all the time. The knowledge and proof of God is known by the Spirit. We are spirits; to have no spiritual awareness is foolish and it's embarrassing, actually. God is Spirit, we are spirits, to have no knowledge of the existence of God has to make a person ask if they, themselves actually exist.

A man can have whatever he says. God deals with all of us according to who we are, how we believe. If/when that man gets to hell, and he sees that God is **not** there he will believe that he was right all along. Unless he can look past the chasm that is between Heaven and Hell and be tremendously disappointed to find out that he has been wrong all the time.

This agnostic can be so prideful that he cannot admit that he cannot commit because perhaps he's too fearful that he will be wrong. Pride will also keep a man from humbling himself under the mighty hand of God and asking God for anything … food, protection, health--, Salvation.

By not acknowledging and then accepting God, man by default, because of being in the Earth is serving the devil. No one is neutral, everyone is serving God or not-God. It's not like a text message that you can opt out of. Man will serve one or the other, one way or the other. Most often the man who believes he's living his own life and serving *himself* is really serving the devil. The man who is serving himself is serving the devil because the devil is the *god* of the unsaved man's flesh.

Ancestral Worship

Ancestral worship is the custom of venerating deceased ancestors who are considered still a part of the family and whose spirits are believed to have the power to intervene in the affairs of the living. **Many people think their dead relatives have become angels; they have not.** They are not watching over you; they are not helping you out because the dead know nothing. Some believe that the dead are still here walking around with the power to influence or protect them while they continue to live their life. This is an open invitation to a *familiar spirit, guardian demon* and/or *spirit spouse*, which may all be the same entity.

Jesus said, **Greater things you will do because I go to My Father,** (John 14:12). No human in the Bible ever said that or is able to do that.

Ancestral worship is a way for you to describe to the demonic world what you are looking for, give them the idea of the person that you will accept–, so these demons can impersonate and masquerade as that person and present to you in the dream or in some other way to "advise" you and basically lead you astray or gain entrance or further foothold into your mind and life to derail you, run you crazy, or turn you away from destiny.

Oh, but it's not just dead ancestors. How many dead celebrities are people still celebrating? This is not of God. It lends itself to idol worship and invites *familiar spirits, guardian demons*, and *spirit spouses,* among other styled demons.

Demonic Adornment

Demonic adornments include demonic tattoos and jewelry. Clothing style and choices can garner demonic attention and attract demons to your life.

Adornments such as hair coloring are indicative of the evil marine kingdom, such as pink, green, or blue hair and variations of those colors, especially rainbow-colored hair. You are inviting demons into your life.

Demons can put an unseen spiritual mark on people so that they are treated in a certain way by other *spirits* and also in the natural by humans. It's usually a mark of reproach and rejection.

When you choose demonic attire, makeup, hairdos, you mark yourself –, well there you go.

The announcement of your arrival may offend others, but many are not offended by it. If you dress scantily, cleavage up and out, tight, tight Monistat jeans, Daisey Dukes, and short, short skirts you will attract people, but you will attract people who have certain *spirits* – the **spirit of lust** comes to mind.

This is not always the case. A person with a lusty spirit doesn't need visual stimuli they are already demonically charged, but a person who has that spirit, for example now SEES something they like to look at, well – there you go, again.

Demonic and witchcraft décor items in the home attract evil *spirits*. If you have a natural affinity for all things witchy, you may *be* a witch. If you don't want to be delivered from witchcraft expect all the things FROM GOD that witches get. If you didn't know and were just decorating in the latest style, but it was witchy or demonic, then get rid of that stuff. Don't give it away, burn it or completely destroy it so no one else can use it.

Festivals

Festivals and concerts are not all innocent. Seriously, some bands are demonic. Concertgoers are subject to what comes through the microphone and over the speakers. Some "artists" are demonic, demonized, channeling--, hey it makes them look different, edgy, and sound good, but at what cost?

Song and music covenants are made.

Dance covenants are made.

Curses can be made and ratified when you sing, you are still using the spoken word. It is the same as praying, except you are praying to music, and or to a beat. Once committed to memory, you may pray the same word blessings or curses over and again for years or even decades. It all depends on if those words are of God or not.

A man shall have what he says, (Mark 11:23)

Eastern Star/Freemasons

The foothold of Freemasons in the world today is astounding; there are about 6 million with 2 million in the Northern Hemisphere. Originally, the Freemason's was advertised as a men's only fraternity and it is an oathbound, secret society. They claim to be devoted to fellowship and moral discipline, mutual assistance, but it is completely demonic.

The children of Freemasons suffer more than the Freemasons themselves because a lot of the secret oaths require the swearing of devastating things to happen to themselves AND their children if they divulge Freemason secrets, their oaths, secrets, and words. Secret clubs to me are like a 10-year-old little boys club house, only with demons. This isn't child's play, these people use blood, and they use grown men who are accountable for what they say. Freemasons are basically selling out their kids, probably while being told that being a Freemason will make things better for their kids.

It is the world's largest secret society, and they conceal their rituals. They agree to tormenting illness and death if they tell Freemason secrets. That should give anyone--, especially a grown man pause, before uttering such evil from his mouth. Unless that man is unspiritual, immature, desperate, drunk – whatever -- . unless he's unsaved and doesn't know any better. Unless he's UNFAITHFUL and does not believe that his own words will have any weight or come to pass.

And if/when these devastations come to pass WHO do they think will enforce these punishments? The devil, of course. (I hope they are not blaming this on God, because that would be blasphemy on top of everything else.)

Ironic that many who are in the group are not even brick masons but by joining the group freedom is what is lost, not found.

The sister organization of the Freemasons is the Eastern Star.

College fraternities and sororities are the training grounds for Freemasons and make the same type of oaths and maybe even the same oaths in some cases. They are secret societies with branding, secret words, secret handshakes. Those who pledge and swear into these societies may do so unto death. It is possible to renounce membership of fraternities and sororities but getting out of the Freemasons requires a lot more spiritual work.

Fraternities

How many movies have been made a college fraternities and sororities? A fraternity (frat) is an organized group of people with a common purpose, interest or pleasure. The college frats are commonly formed for social purposes. They pretend or believe that they are connected to do good in the community or the world--, oh please. They party.

It is a boys' club, I mean, men's club which is a social club.

These first Black fraternities and sororities are called the Divine Nine. I don't agree with that nomenclature; there is nothing divine about inducing teens and 20-something year olds to pledge and bow down to idol *gods* and not even tell them that is what they are doing.

- Alpha Phi Alpha Fraternity, 1906, Cornell University.
- Alpha Kappa Alpha Sorority, 1908, Howard University.
- Kappa Alpha Psi Fraternity, 1911, Indiana University.
- Omega Psi Phi Fraternity, 1911, Howard
- Delta Sigma Theta Sorority, 1913, Howard

Either knowingly, but most often unknowingly the pledges and hazing to join a frat are traumatic, dehumanizing and demonic. They pledge oaths to Roman *gods*, Greek *gods* and their Egyptian equivalents. This is all very spiritually dangerous. Here's an idea of what and who they pledge to that drags even a saved person into polytheism which is paganism. A man (woman) cannot serve two masters. Pledging a frat or sorority drags a person into idolatry.

- **Phi Kappa psi – make oaths to Apollo.**
- **Alpha Phi Alpha** – worship the Sphinx and or Hecate
- **Phi Beta Sigma** – Athena
- **Omega Psi Phi** – We think Anubis because they call themselves dogs, but Apollo is on

their crest in the feminine version. Asherah, Semiramus, Diana (Gr.), the "Mother Goddess" Queen of Heaven.

The Egyptian equivalent of Hecate is Nephthys, she is the **mother goddess of witchcraft, death, burial, darkness, and mourning**. She is the mother of the dog-headed *god of hell*, Anubis. **Omega Psi Phi** is associated with Anubis, the Egyptian mythological false *god* with a head of a jackal. He relates to the embalming of the dead. Anubis was involved with the Underworld in Egyptian mythology.

Iota Phi Theta – Their patron *god* seems to be Nimrod's son, Tammuz, the centaur.

See Reginald Paige's YouTube channel for much more information on Fraternities and Sororities and their involvement with false *gods*. *Gods of the Divine 9.*

https://www.youtube.com/watch?v=EmHGKxx3h 60&t=28s

Irreligion

Irreligion is indifference to, hostility to religion or lack of religious belief. Anti-Christ rules the heart of the person who is hostile to God.

Atheism is not believing in any *god* while agnosticism is doubting the existence of God. Both these groups are seen as *irreligious*. You're also irreligious if you do believe in God but don't belong to a religious group or attend religious services.

Relative to its populations the top 5 countries with the highest number of agnostics and atheists are Sweden, Vietnam, Denmark, Norway, and Japan. Haiti is 11% irreligious; I mention it because Vodun is their main religion.

The religiously unaffiliated now make up just over one quarter of the U.S. population. Most people in this category believe in God or some higher power and describe themselves as **"spiritual but not religious,"** (SBNR).

I am more inclined to believe I'm meeting people who believe in *religion* but by no fault of their own they have **not met God**. Either because of culture, tradition, or lack of a real teaching church that walks in the five-fold ministry gifts they are suffering demonic oppression, attacks and a defeated life.

(I'm coining this phrase now: RBNS, they are *Religious But Not Spiritual*.)

The final group who are neither religious nor spiritual--, well Jesus said, The poor you will have with you always. Keep being irreligious if you like, God will find you irrelevant when you call on Him.

Judaism/Kabbalah Tree

The Kabbalah Tree is mystical in origin. Do your own research regarding it. Jews missed Jesus while He was right there in the flesh with them, right in front of them. They hated Him and killed Him. These same folks get most of their teaching through ancient texts such as the Talmud and a lot of that is based on the Kabbalah Tree.

There is a lot of research out there about SRA and somehow that Kabbalah Tree is integral to their ritualistic abuse.

Magic (Magick)

Magick is the use of "energy" to effect changes in a person's life. This word, *magick* or it's more updated version, *magic* is associated with witches, wicca, and wiccans.

Magic employs powers of the supernatural. God does not deal in magic. The powers they invoke are of the 2nd heaven, which is Satan's territory. Rulers of wickedness in high places are there and are used to bewitch others, to conjure up devils and demons, to enchant or cast a spell. These spells invoke supernatural powers. Know there are principalities, rulers and powers in high places – namely the second heaven. This is not free "energy" that is out there for your command; it is demons.

A person enchanting magic is calling on dark powers, even if they have a Bible sitting right in front of them. I've heard stories of dark priests running to get a Bible when the evil they've summoned up runs over them and they are afraid.

They should be afraid.

There is no genie (ginnie, djinn, jinn) in a bottle to grant wishes. Genies are spirits of Arabian folklore, and frequently depicted as being imprisoned in a bottle or lamp that can grant wishes when summoned. What an enticement. The only problem is they don't go back into the bottle, and they don't live in bottles, unless bottles are the new *tiny houses* of HELL.

A dark power enchanter may invoke the powers of the moon (moon magic), sun (sun magic) stars, water – somehow, they've found a way to use most if not all of the elements of the Earth including trees, stones, dirt, fire, and/or wind, against mankind.

Magic as entertainment is also dangerous because the magicians are wizards and less often witches. In order to do their magic tricks somehow they blind you to see only what they want you to see or suspend everyone for just the right amount of time that the audience doesn't really notice they've been suspended, but they accomplish their tricks, akin to hypnosis. Giving oneself over to hypnosis is dangerous and virtue can be stolen in those moments.

New Age

New Age is vague because it keeps getting repackaged and re-presented to make the next generation and the next generation accept it. I remember first hearing the term in the 1980's so why it is still considered *new*, I don't know. But it keeps getting repackaged, I suppose it gets spiritual Botox injections to keep looking fresh to new converts and victims.

Young people love to think that they are doing something new, original, something that they think their parents are not hip to. The devil, a master marketer knows this. New Ageism is an alternative approach to "religion." It is spirituality but it is not God and is not *of* God. It is old stuff made new again. It is still Mysticism, Holism and Environmentalism.

Here are some things that are really New Age, some with brief definitions. If you are doing ANY of this, you are inviting demons into your life. Do you see why we haven't prayed yet, and why knowledge must be given first?

Affirmations without God- will always include the devil.

Aliens – Fascination with other lifeforms can open you to demons pretending to be aliens, or aliens pretending to be people.

Angel Cards – Demons disguised as angels, use truth and lies, to hook you and lead you to deception.

Angel Numbers – New Age observers have decided that numbers that show up repeatedly are not coincidental; rather, they are messages from angels. Problem is these are demons disguised as angels.

Angel Readings –nowhere in the Bible does it say we should call on angels to tell our future.

Angel Worship – Angelology. People who believe in Earth Angels, the **worship** of **angels** (or angelolatry. We do not seek angels or pray to angels. If what you believe to be an angel receives your worship then it is demonic and of the devil. The devil wants worship. An angel of God will say as he did to John, "See that you do it not."

Ascended Masters –Some believe that deceased religious leaders and mythical beings can be contacted for guidance. These are all demons. The dead know nothing.

Astral Projection – the ability of a person to leave their body, travel to a distant place and then return to their body at will. I will add, while they are in this distant place they can accomplish certain things, usually evil things.

Astro cartography – Using astrology to decide where to live is likely to steer you away from God's will for your living situation.

Astrology –Horoscopes. For years I've thought that if there are 12 zodiac signs, then there are only

12 types of people in the world. Either that's a lie and/or horoscopes are lies.

Automatic Writing – is allowing a demon, usually a *lying spirit* to flow through your hands to write onto a piece of paper. The purpose is to send you in wrong directions, derail your life. It is a *familiar spirit* who will most often tell you what you already believe or want to hear.

Candles- Lighting and burning candles with intention. Even if your intention is good – to get money, a man, for healing—is invoking the devil. Jesus said to ask what you will, and **He** will give it to you. He didn't say to go through a lot of rituals and foolishness to make things happen.

Casting Spells

Casting a spell by use of words thought to be magic, especially to have an effect on something or someone else makes you a witch/warlock, plain and simple. Unless you repent immediately you have everything coming to you FROM GOD that witches have coming to them.

Thou shalt not suffer a witch to live.

Exodus 22:18

Chanting. Enchanting. Casting spells. Just for fun, just to see what will happen. Or you don't believe it so you're making a mockery of God--, you have everything coming to your FROM GOD that witches have coming to them. As well your children will now be born into witchcraft. Don't expect to have any peace from demonic oppression and demons coming at you day and night if not now, eventually.

> But the cowardly, the unbelieving, the vile, the murderers, the sexually immoral, **those who practice magic arts,** the idolaters and all liars—they will be consigned to the fiery lake of burning sulfur. This is the second death. Revelation 21:8

(emphasis added, mine)

There are other kinds of spells as well – potion spells, food spells, beverage spells, so many different kinds. River spells, water spells, rock spells, Earth spells, dirt and sand spells, air spells… if only man would use that knowledge and imagination for good rather than evil.

Chakras – A chakra is a spiritual "power point" in (on) the body, used in Yoga and Eastern mysticism. These "mystics" have convinced people that whatever is wrong with them is because their *chakras* are out of balance. So, going to have one's "chakras balanced" is not of God. My pressing question is, how did the chakras get out of balance in the first place?

Channeling -it's like a séance for one, this can be called, *reaching out to demons.*

Christ Consciousness – Do not believe every spirit but test the *spirits* to see whether they are from God, because many false prophets have gone out into the world.

Course in Miracles – A *channeled* book, supposedly dictated by Jesus.

Crystals – there are people who believe in the power of crystals. This is not of God.

Crystal Balls

Crystal balls and fortune tellers at the beach is not fun on vacation. It is seeking a diviner. Saul, when he was cut off by God did this and was dead shortly after. You may say you did this, and nothing happened. Really? **How do you know that you didn't die spiritually that very day, that very hour?** Oh, you're still alive and ½ the time your body is vertical, so you think you're alive.

Adam and Eve were vertical in the Garden of Eden after they sinned. Do you think God would tell them that if they ate of the only tree that he told them not to eat of because they would die that they wouldn't actually die? God is not a joke. God is not a pushover. God is not a liar.

You can't trick God. So why are you still alive? Maybe you're not. This is where we need to know more spiritual things – God can keep you alive. But if you are not dwelling in safety, peace, abundance, and prosperity you may already be spiritually dead. If the favor and the glory of God has left your life, you may already be spiritually dead. Today may be a good day to receive Salvation in Jesus Christ –, while you have breath, while you're vertical, while you're on *this side*.

Let's put it this way, if the devil has the ability to kill the body and the soul, in hell and a man can be captive and in hell while he is still here in the Earth… once captured, if the devil has control of your soul, does he not also have control over your *life*?

Cults are organizations that do not serve God but some other deity. Sometimes the leader is the "deity." People think these are religions, but they are cults:

1. The Church of Jesus Christ of Latter-Day Saints.
2. The Watchtower and Jehovah's Witnesses.
3. The Church of Scientology
4. The Holy Spirit Association for the Unification of World Christianity.
5. The International Churches of Christ.
6. The Family.
7. Christian Identity Movement, KKK
8. The Nation of Islam
9. UPC
10. People's Temple
11. Heaven's Gate
12. *And others…*

Deities and Divinities

Divination -Divining or divination is the practice of attempting to foresee the future by the interpretation of signs or omens by use of supernatural powers, intuition, ESP, clairvoyance or by some other occultic practice.

God states He will not do anything without first revealing His plans to His prophets. When mankind wants to go around God, he develops occultic methods to try to know the future. People get caught up in this because sometimes none of it is true. Sometimes ½ of it is true. Misleading a man can ruin his entire life. Folks could end up marrying the wrong person, dropping out of school, moving to the wrong city or country, or even quitting the right job. Not being in the right place at the right time could cancel a man's destiny.

Dowsing is a type of divination employed in attempts to locate ground water, buried metals, gemstones, oil, via "earth vibrations" and many other objects without the use of a scientific apparatus.

Dream Catchers

Drumming Circles- going into trances is not safe and it is not of God.

Energy Healing – Craniosacral manipulation. Reiki, and other "Healing" Arts. Cranial **Sacral** Therapy **is** Based on New Age **God**, Aka; and it is scientifically unfounded, dangerous,

Acupuncture is from Chinese medicine. Only about 4% of Chinese people are saved. Most practice Chinese folk religions and their medicine types reflect that.

I'm embarrassed and transparent enough to say I've tried some of these things and I do not recommend you bring any of this into your life. For one thing, when a person is oppressed or in pain acutely or chronically, he/she may resort to uncommon methods. By my trying acupuncture or other Chinese arts it was as though I was tested like Job, and I failed. I did not curse God verbally, but did I go to a strange altar to receive of that altar? Lord, forgive me.

Jesus is my Healer, and my spirit man should have been strong enough to stand on that.

Was I healed by Chinese medicine? Know this: The devil can "heal" by *appearing* to heal. He can take away the pain or symptoms ***temporarily***, usually by hiding them somewhere else in the body or relieving the symptoms for a while and then they will surface again. I've heard of cases where the disorder or disease is transferred to someone else. Better stay prayed up, **even in deliverance and healing services.**

National surveys conducted in the early 21st century estimated that some 80% of the population of China, which is more than a billion people, practice some kind of Chinese folk religion; 15% are Buddhists; 10% are Taoist; **2.5% are Christians**; and 1% are Muslims. How can you get saved, and expect God-focused healing arts from unsaved people? I guess I'm asking myself that, too.

Entity Group – Supposedly a collection of *spirits* who speak through channelers.

Dwarves (mystical creatures), not small people. They are evil and can appear as *children* in the dream, but they are fully grown demons.

Elves, dwarves and fairies exist and are all evil. A lot of the lesser demons appear as short little things like three or four feet tall.

Fairies – Evil entities that do exist. Some people seek out fairies to know what they should do next. The Tooth Fairy is a form of worship of fairies. Leaving the tooth under the pillow is a form of offering, bowing to that altar.

Feng Shui – more energy talk. Singing bowls are a part of this. Tibetans believe that vibrations affect energy. Show me that in the Bible, please?

Flower of Life – is a form of sacred geometry which Judaism uses. It is not Christian although it is in some Christian texts. It is part of the Kabbalah Tree which is found in Freemason texts for example.

Follow Your Heart (or Believe; Follow Your Dreams; Follow Your Bliss; etc.)

Fortune Telling – (see also Divination) **Runes – another form of fortunetelling.** The throwing rocks, sticks, stones, bones… throwing entrails of dead animals and then "reading" how they land is no more than a person listening to a familiar spirit as they perform a ritual. This invites demons into your life.

Coffee Grounds reading, Tea Leaf reading, Palm readers. People will even read the nodes on your head if you let them.

Goddess worship will invite all kinds of demons into your life.

Graveyards. Don't hang out at funerals or graveyards, especially if you're not prayed up.

Harry Potter –taught children and adults how to do witchcraft. The author has been paid handsomely *in this life* for that. But there is Eternity to look at.

Horoscopes –see Divination.

Hypnosis –Losing voluntary consciousness by suggestion of a hypnotist. Not of God. Not recommended. Anything could be introduced into your life at that time.

Idols – The people of God get into the MOST trouble for idolatry than for almost anything else. Read your Bible, it's too much to summarize in a sentence or two.

Mental Journeying – Shamans sometimes facilitate this.

Law of Attraction – Believing that you are attracting things with your focused energy is most likely you are sending demons out to get things for you.

Mandalas – a geometric figure representing the universe in Hindu and Buddhist symbolism. More layering of "religions". No other religion is to e mixed with Christianity. That is worshipping at strange altars.

Manifesting - Using thoughts, feelings, and beliefs to bring something to our physical reality—willing demons, as above.

Meditating *without* **God** –

Mediumship – Leaders of seances and channelers are called mediums. They are *spiritists*.

Mercury Retrograde – is related to Astrology where a person believes there are some things that you should never do when Mercury is retrograde because it is not good for "luck."

Metatron's Cube – Supposedly the "sacred geometry" held by an angel named Metatron (who is mentioned in Jewish legend, but not in the Holy

Bible). This is part of the Kabbalah Tree, which is used in Judaism, and also Freemasonry.

Numerology – is the study of numbers and their effect on our lives. No where in the Bible is this done or said to be done. It is a form of fortune telling and used often in gambling circles.

When applied to a person's name it is a form of onomancy. You can find this and other related types of New Ageism on social media platforms masquerading as **games**. That's the same as the devil calling your name and you answering him. **STOP IT!** STOP letting yourself be initiated into occultism.

Occultism -believing in supernatural forces or beings--, magical or divinatory. Belief in the existence of secret, mysterious, or supernatural agencies, the practice of the occult arts. *Occult* means *dark* or *hidden.*

OMG – Saying the Lord's name in vain violates the Third Commandment. If I use this term, I really mean it and I say, I really mean that I am calling on the Name of the Lord.

Oomancy – Divination by eggs.

Oracle Cards – people use these with Tarot. It's hard for me to think that everything that can happen in a person's life can be in a deck of so many cards and you just shuffle them, and they lay out the future for you. Ridiculous when you think about it.

Out-of-Body Experiences

Paganism -Paganism is believing in ancient religions such as there is a *god* for everything; that is called polytheism. I am changing the dictionary/encyclopedic definition to say that paganism is practicing religions *other than* **Protestant Christianity**. I am saying that because Catholics pray to all kinds of "saints" that are no more than renamed ***African pagan gods*** brought here with them when African slavery became a thing in this hemisphere. That is idolatry.

I will say again: Every time you think you are getting something for nothing, something evil may be introduced into your life, or SOMETHING IS BEING TAKEN AWAY FROM YOU. Or both; it is an old devil trick.

Pantheism – believing that everyone and everything is a *god*. These people use the word, *universe* often. They describe God as the universe.my Bible say God created the Earth and world, not God *became the Earth and world.*

Past-Life Regression – by use of hypnosis a person is taken back into their past or allegedly into a past life. Obviously, there is belief in reincarnation which is **not** of God. Most likely, there's that old *familiar spirit* making up some stuff or telling you about the past people it lived *through.*

Peace Signs – A peace sign is an upside-down and broken cross, symbolizing rebellion against Christianity. That symbol says, Peace, peace when there is no peace.

Pendulums – a swinging rope or string with an object on the end to indicate yes or no to a Yes-or-No-type question. (Not the same as Urim and Thummin from the Bible.)

Polytheism – Serving or worshipping multiple "gods." Fraternities and Sororities induce their pledges and initiates to do this. Whether they realize it or not, they are still WRONG, WRONG, WRONG. This is idolatry.

Power Animals – are considered "spiritual helpers" in animal form. It is said that you can invoke the assistance of your power animal when you need help. The shaman is known for this pagan behavior.

Psychic Readings – a person may go to a psychic for the purpose of obtaining information from a person who has heightened spiritual ability. Usually, this ability comes from the 2nd Heaven, the devil's domain.

Prophetic Words from God are genuine and come from the 3rd Heaven.

Sacred Geometry- is superstition in my opinion where it gives sacred meanings to certain geometric shapes especially if a person is wearing that geometric shape. See **Flower of Life**.

Shamanism –animism. A medium who uses trances and invokes power animals to advise people. A shaman is a person regarded as having access to, and influence in, the world of good and evil *spirits* to practice divination and "healing."

Sorcery – The use of black magic.

Spells – either casting them yourself or asking or paying someone to do them for you is still witchcraft. Even so-called protection spells and rituals with sage or smudging is demonic. It calls up demons instead of protecting you from them. Only Salvation in Jesus Christ can protect you from these evils. No demon is going to protect you from another demon. Certain incense or incense with intention does the same thing.

Spirit Animal - Spirit Animals are animal spirit guides who allegedly offer love, strength, support, inspiration, and guidance. --, this is not of God.

Spirit Guides – Guardian demons do not mean you any good. We are all assigned a guardian angel when we are born, but over time if we keep doing evil, running to evil, sinning and living a dark life the guardian angel will be replaced with a guardian demon. The guardian demon's job is to run your life down to hell if possible.

Statues – Lends itself to idolatry as God told us to make no graven image of Him.

Sweat Lodges – Uh. Connect with *God* by overheating, sweating and possibly not having enough oxygen? No. A sweat lodge is a sauna on steroids.

Tapping – Emotional Freedom Technique based on the Eastern concept of chi and meridians, or pathways of energy flow within the body. There's that word, *energy* again.

Tarot Cards – Man ever wants to know the future when the Bible says give no thought for tomorrow. So, he has tried to find ways to find out the future by fortune telling. Note that it is called fortune telling, not misfortune telling, so you can guess everything will be flowery and nice. Prophesy to us lightly. If there is any drama to anything that is told it is to alarm the listener and to probably get money or other gifts from the victim who came to this fortunetelling meeting.

A tarot deck is usually 78 cards with pictures that supposedly can foretell someone's future. These cards were originally from the 15th century Europe for playing card games.

Some card readers use regular playing cards.

Totems – family totems, are idolatrous and not of God. They can be seen in both African and Eskimo cultures.

Unicorns – Are bad if they symbolize magic.

Universalism – The belief that everyone goes to heaven.

Universe – some people don't call God's name but call Him the Universe. They also believe the Universe is God.

Wicca – Wicca is a neo-pagan religion.

Witchcraft – to include Conjuration, Folk Magic, Mojo, Voodoo, Vodoun, Hoodoo, Roots, Santeria, Obeah, (Obayi), both African spellcasting and healing traditions found in the Caribbean.

Multiple types of witchcraft practiced worldwide by Witchdoctors, herbalists, healers, sangomas.

Witchtok- social media's alive with demonic things that normalize wrong and evil. Some call the name of "God" while they are divining, confusing people even more. I'm not sure which God they mean, and some have CHRISTIAN music playing in the background while they fake proph-a-lie. So many are deceived.

So, don't get caught up in it.

Zodiac Signs – I repeat from the Horoscope section: For years I've thought that if there are 12 zodiac signs, then there are only 12 types of people in the world. Ludicrous.

Pagan Holidays

Some pagan holidays are dressed up, masquerading as Christian holidays. Some pagan holidays are nude and streaking through the streets, boldly, uninhibited, not pretending to be anything other than a pagan holiday--, just doing their thing.

Participating in them says you agree with them, and you are worshipping the same *god* or *gods* that their devotees worship. You are adding your grace to this and possibly forming an evil alliance that you may not know that you need to get out of until years from now. Or, you may never know what hardship you have laid on your children and your children's children as they are blindsided with delays, barrenness, evil spiritual oppressions and attack for no cause of their own.

All because you participated or had them to participate, initiating them into that dark world.

<u>Rituals</u>

What saddens me is that Jesus already came to Earth, taught masterfully and all of Jerusalem missed His visitation. The Bible is written down for our edification, duplicated, exegeted, broken down, taught, weekly all over the world, written about and 2200 years later we haven't gotten the message as to what is **idolatry** and what is Godly worship of the Only Living God and what the outcome(s) will be for those who never make covenant with God; those who violate covenant and don't repent and for those who are so narcissistic they won't even acknowledge that God *is*.

Rituals can initiate a person into witchcraft or other forms of darkness unbeknownst to them. This is why we need to study to show ourselves approved. This is why we need to know the tactics of the enemy and do not give in to them.

Online when it says, *"Click here for a free ---- whatever,"* and you do it. That click signs you up for 3 years of something you don't want and can't get out of. With the devil, it's the same, but worse. And eternal.

We can't continue clueless.

Lord, help us all.

Shriners

Shriners International, formally known as the Ancient Arabic Order of the Nobles of the Mystic Shrine (AAONMS), is an American Masonic society established in 1870 and is headquartered in Tampa, Florida.

Make of that what you will.

They have hospitals and they help children.

And?

Make of that what you will.

Sororities

A sorority is a woman's student organization chiefly at colleges and universities. It is the girl's version of a fraternity. It is supposed to look like a group of people coming together to do good. The hazing is ridiculous, why would you need to eat dog food to do good in the community. It's all a lie.

But they must pledge, and many times hazed and make oaths to strange *gods* that are not Yahweh, our God, the Only Living God. Their crests usually show Greek, Roman, and Egyptian *gods* and their symbols. This is who they are pledging to, and it is serious. This can derail their entire Christian life and their entire natural life and the lives of their family,

Kappa Alpha Psi has Thoth (*god* of wisdom) in their rituals.

Zeta Psi Beta has the false cat *god* of Bastet (or the Devouring lady).

AKA -Their coat of arms has the Greek mythological Titan Atlas holding up the world.

Some of these groups kneel on shrines to false *gods*. The altar of Kappa Alpha Psi is placed in the center of the room and covered with a crimson and cream coverlet. The same was used as the shrine of the false *god*, Apollo (in the Greek polytheistic religion). The pledges bow to the altar. Surely there is a spiritual experience, but it is not of God. **Everything is spiritual because we are spirits, but everything spiritual is not of God.** This is why we have to discern *spirits* and know the difference.

Sigma Gamma Rho refers to Ma'at and the Divine Serpent as its inspiration.

The Deltas embrace Minerva, the goddess of wisdom. The **Spirit of Wisdom** was with **God** in the beginning. (Read the Book of Proverbs.) Minerva is a false, Roman *goddess* whose name is Athena in Greek mythology, and neither are to be praised. Minerva's Egyptian equivalent is Neith.

Deltas also worship Hecate and Daphne who is Anat in Egyptian lore, the lover of Nimrod.

National Pan-Hellenic Council, Inc. is an umbrella group of nine African American Greek fraternities and sororities called the Divine Nine and there is nothing divine about worshipping Roman, Greek, or Egyptian *gods* and *goddesses*. It is polytheism, pantheism. Perhaps by using the prefix, PAN- they realized what they were doing all along. Pantheism is a doctrine which identifies God with the universe or regards the universe as a manifestation of God. It is also worship that admits or tolerates all *gods*.

If ignorantly they think they just formed some social clubs and then got mascots to make them look cool, scholarly, or have an attractive crest for their logos, they missed the mark terribly as it will come to judgment by a Most Holy God who says to have NO OTHER GODS BEFORE ME, and constantly reminds us in the Bible not to bow to other *gods*.

I have not met one African American who came from Rome or Greece so why they'd serve these pagan *gods* is beyond me. Egyptian *gods* are older and have been repackaged many, many times so being of African descent they could be serving pagan gods that they don't even know about down their bloodline. But to go to college to be educated but to be tricked into a dumbing down into idolatry is grievous.

Catholics are praying to African *gods* as these *gods* masquerade as Catholic saints to garner worship, and they are getting that worship.

Catholics are the main group calling and asking for deliverance. Of course, they call it *exorcism* which is done by a priest. Catholics who are religious but not spiritual need to meet God and get saved. **Deliverance is the Protestant Christian's bread.**

Sigma Gamma Rho was created in 1922. Helene Previl was once a leader in that sorority, ΣΓΡ. A sorority or fraternity is an organized group that is composed of **pagan** beliefs, plus rituals, she said. Their stated purpose is to prepare young individuals to *continue the legacy of* **secret societies** via brainwashing and subliminal mind control. Much brainwashing is involved in such organizations.

Helene has compared pagan Haitian Voodoo rituals to the rituals she performed as a member of that sorority, that were *similar* to those done in the practice of Voodoo.

Voodoo (Vodun) is a powerful form of witchcraft. **Know that all forms of witchcraft are powerful if unopposed**. The goal of the witch is to remain occult, that is *hidden* and therefore unopposed, taking their victim by surprise.

This is why we have to stay prayed up. Surprise attacks.

Ms. Previl said that she was required to repeat the oath constantly. This would be to brainwash and get that doctrine deep into the mind of the pledge.

Alpha Kappa Alpha (Daughters of Minos and Bacchus who in my opinion is THE party *god; he is* named Dionysius in Greek mythology is the *god* of *wine* and pleasure. Hecate's wheel on their crest is a labyrinth. In mythology, Minos a minotaur would eat 7 boys and 7 girls who were lost in a maze. A part of the AKA's pledge is to state something about wandering in life, through a maze, repeating it 7 times. These are **word curses** that they are willingly, ignorantly speaking over themselves and their lives. **Why**? Lord Jesus, *why*?

Zeta Phi Beta's hear in their initiations that Baselius Zeta has been written on your hearts and minds. You are ready to receive the light of Zeta. More idolatry. Jesus is the LIGHT of the world, not these idol *gods* of Greece, Rome, and Egypt.

It saddens me that frats and sororities are based on ancient mythology and idol worship and that young people and sometimes those of grad chapters still fall for this.

These pledges all tie their souls to the groups they join. A tied soul cannot prosper.

Oaths are a form of swearing. Swear not.

(Read my books on Soul Prosperity).

Superstitions

A belief or practice done because of fear, ignorance, fear of the unknown, trusting in chance, magic, or false cause and effect is superstition. A superstition is an irrational attitude toward the supernatural, nature, or God. Doing things that make no sense when it's been proven false. There are many people who have a collection of superstitions even though they've all been proven false. Sadly, they are quick to pass these old wives' tales on to their children rather than truth. There is usually alarm and other emotions attached to these fears, so the person is more likely trying to protect his loved ones by what he knows, which is leaning on his own understanding instead of asking God.

Things having to do with ladders, black cats and the like may come to mind. Mostly due to the fear of the unknown, especially as it relates to religion, people do ritualistic and nonsensical things. Throwing salt over your shoulder is one of these rituals. Please don't let me catch you throwing cinnamon out your front door. If you drink margaritas, you might have salt in a plate in your house. If you live off the grid and you are salt curing a ham in your smokehouse that might be another reason to have salt in a dish, other than that, you are practicing witchcraft. Lemons under the bed, whole eggs in water, the list goes on. It is witchcraft, and it initiates the person performing the ritual into witchcraft. This opens the door for the demons you are trying to get rid of.

If you are not aware that you are a witch or have become a witch, you are a *blind witch*. If you become a witch, then your children are now witches. Automatically.

Satanism

Satanism began with the atheistic Church of Satan founded by Anton LaVey in the United States in 1966.

Satanism is an obsession with, or affinity for evil specifically the worship of Satan, marked by the travesty of Christian rites.

Many people believe that Satan and God have the same power; **they don't**. Satan was created by God. Satan was an angel named Lucifer, but he fell from Heaven and was renamed Satan. He is a fallen angel.

Angels don't have the same power as God and certainly fallen angels do not have the same power as GOD.

Luciferianism

Luciferianism is a system of belief which involves black magick (magic) in its worship of Lucifer and other so-called deities usually in the pursuit of power. **It is evil spiritual interference.** Luciferic beings have plagued humanity along with the destructive evil beings.

You know how they say you *are* what you eat? You get what you worship. You worship Satan/Lucifer you will get demons.

Séances

Séances conjure up demons. *WHY*?

A séance is a meeting held by a spiritist (medium) to receive spirit communications to convince another or others that the spiritist has called up a ghost. It is a meeting to get messages from the spirits of a **dead person** or **dead people**.

Saul got a witch to try to reach dead Samuel in the Bible. The witch called up a *familiar spirit* which pretended to be Samuel. Days later, Saul was DEAD.

Calling up a *familiar spirit* and basically telling it how you want it to appear – as a dead relative for example, then accepting whatever lying words the *spiritist* either hears or pretends to hear does not show a lot of Wisdom. It may indicate a broken heart, over emotionality, or a broken spirit. Here comes a demon with its lying words. Usually after that, the victim pays--, in more ways than one.

Whether the spiritist knows this is fake or not depends on the spiritist. These are real spiritual events; there could be a heaviness in the atmosphere, there could be goosebumps, you could get a chill-- but it doesn't mean it's **from God**. You must practice discernment and practice your relationship with God to know when God is present or when He is not, and some other *entity* or *entities* are present.

Ouija board, *familiar spirits, monitoring spirits, guardian demons* all imitate this séance type meeting.

Now the séance is over. This conjured up demon will go where now? Back to sleep? Back to hell? Haven't thought about that have you? It may follow you home. I mean it is accepted now; you've even invited it to speak. How will you get rid of it? You could get rid of a stray cat that you've fed already easier than it will be to send this demon back to hell.

Any Religion Other Than Protestant Christianity

Don't think that because I didn't mention what you do, or what your family has traditionally done that you are off the hook. I don't know everything, but I've shared what I do know right now. If what you do is NOT in the Bible as accepted Christian practice, it is demonic. If it clearly shows that a practice was demonic in Bible times, then it is still demonic now. And, if Jesus Christ is not in it, if it is any "religion" other than Protestant Christianity, it is most likely of the devil and opening doors that you really do not want open.

Anything you do with regularity and intention is a religion. Anything you do with regularity and intention circumventing God, cutting God out of the picture is a religion, and it is idolatry.

The only way to God is through Jesus Christ. The only way to Heaven is through Jesus Christ. The only way to bliss, nirvana or whatever you call Peace, Joy and Happiness is in the Holy Spirit of God and that by Jesus Christ. The Holy Spirit was released in the Earth by Jesus Christ; no one, no other entity has any of that stuff to offer anyone else. Everything else is demons. Period.

Any interactions you are having in the spiritual, may be spiritual but they are demons.

Spiritual is spiritual, but if it's not God via Jesus Christ and in the Holy Spirit it is demons. It is idolatry and you are opening the door for torment and everything else that comes with it and because of it.

Virgin Mary

Praying to Virgin Mary is NOT anywhere in the Holy Bible. The Virgin Mary died. She did not resurrect as Jesus did. Mary was all human, Jesus was born of woman, but He was **all** God. What we know as The Madonna, Mother Mary, the Virgin Mary is a masquerade, it is another name of the Queen of Heaven, Satan's wife. Plus, in the natural, after Jesus, Mary had four more kids, how exactly is she still a virgin? Please tell me.

North and South America: The Western Hemisphere, had you not imported African slaves to build your countries granted you would have missed out on some amazing recipes, but you now have African pagan *gods*. Catholics, you should not be praying to "saints" in the first place, but you've been duped, these are renamed idolatrous, African *gods*. Perhaps the very thing that got the Africans in deep trouble in the first place with God.

You Can't Get There From Here

A soul is under torment and is reaching out for deliverance. As I've said, the problem is without full disclosure, and most people are not being deceitful, people honestly don't know what is real, what is GOD and what is NOT God.

There are some people who are deceitful. A person will work and lie to protect their *gods*. Ironic since their *gods* are supposed to be protecting **them**.

Do folks even know what the Old Testament Laws of God are? I began a list earlier in this book. You can find them all in Exodus 20.

Do people even know what idolatry is? I've shared as much as I can in this book so far. When you participate in idolatry you open every door to your life wide open. God says that when you don't choose Him you choose, by default, the *god* of this world. When you sin, you agree to torments.

You have given permission to the devil to enter your life, and torment you. The devil comes not but to steal, kill and destroy. What will be taken from you? Whatever is most precious to you. Let's start with your peace.

Strange Altars

Idolatry happens when you worship at strange altars. Altars that are not of God with worship that is not to God is idolatrous and opens doors for enemy attack and oppression.

Strange fire is when you are offering up worship that is intended for some other *god,* to God. It's like calling out someone else's name when you are with your spouse.

What You Saw Grandma Do: Traditions

Old wives' tales, superstitions are very dangerous.

Do you want to wait until you're old to find out that the stuff listed in this book is **NOT** how you reach God or serve God? Do not wait until you're old and you're trying to tell people things that they do not understand that you barely understand? Do you want them to think you're crazy?

How many have said that old people "talk out of their head"? Seniors may be saying something that's **both real and true** but if you have no point of reference of what they are talking about, if they have no point of reference because all of their life, they did not believe that this could happen or happen to them then nobody will know what anybody is talking about. Then how can you help Grandma? How can Grandma help you, and her generations, by telling you *what's up* so you can avoid it both now and in your old age?

Whatever you saw Grandma or Grandpa do – whatever they told you--, you must KNOW if it was right, know that it was **of God**. This is not to disrespect Grandma, but you certainly do not want to disrespect God or the Laws of Grace.

Who Do You Think You're Talking To?

That's a demon.

What? What's a demon?

Things that you don't reject but invite or accept in your house, your environment, and into your life, will feel welcome and won't leave. You feel a *presence* in your house one day. You feel like it's Uncle Whomever, because they recently passed, and you miss them. So, you feel enlightened and strike up a conversation with Uncle Whomever. I'll tell you now, whomever you think you are talking to or feeling the *presence* of in your life or environment is **not** your lost relative. It is not a hovering angel from God. It is a demon. That is how they present--, all nice and caring. I mean they don't show up in attack mode. They want to be welcomed. Don't do it.

Spirit Spouse

That's a demon.

What? Again?

For those who are suffering the loss of an interpersonal relationship, mourning, or grieving, you have to really be careful. That "presence" you are feeling ***especially in the night*** is not your lost loved one.

That is a demon.

If you are feeling jewelry on your ring finger especially, or anywhere else, a demon put it there and it thinks it has **married** you. It is a *spirit spouse*. Its goal is to stay with you and your family line forever and block you from having a normal relationship, marriage and family in the natural. If you never marry in the natural, or can't seem to stay married you will not have the chance to bring righteous seed into Earth. Remember, ***Be fruitful and multiply?***

Spirit spouse takes money from you by costing you money, often, strangely. It can bring strange illnesses. Waking up with odd bruises, scratches, or marks on you? *Spirit spouse.* Boyfriends/girlfriends/interpersonal relationships suddenly ending and no one else is noticing you anymore? ***Spirit spouse.***

It blocks blessings so you don't get things you should be getting. I'm not kidding. Start now renouncing it and get rid of it.

Read my book, ***Fantasy Spirit Spouse*** for much more on this.

New Commandment

What is sin? What are the Ten Commandments? Are there other sins? Are there other Commandments?

Jesus gave a New Commandment in the New Testament. And He did that because He could. The Commandments are not over, as long as man may find a loophole to commit sin or as long as the devil finds loopholes to entrap man into sin, curses and death there will be new rules, laws, commandments.

Commandments, like the laws of the Earth, the laws of the road are for our PROTECTION. When the speed limit is 45 in a certain curve on the road that is to protect us, so our car doesn't veer out of control by centrifugal force when trying to corner that turn. Natural laws are for our protection. Gravity, for example, keeps us from floating out into outer space to be lost forever. We obey gravity all the time, we don't step off of mountains or tall buildings. We are very protective of our flesh.

Foremost, we need to obey God; God is trying to protect our spirit (and soul); why don't we obey Him and let Him help us? We obey gravity to the nth degree – if we gain a pound, measured by the Earth's gravitational pull on our body, we go on a diet or hit the gym.

Yeah, we need to obey GOD like that or even more so.

Hopefully now we have a firm grasp on what to do and what not to do, what to stop doing and what to start doing. Most times, it will be a process to get deliverance, but God can do it all at once if He wants and you have the faith. Still, you have to walk out your Christian walk and KEEP your deliverance.

As Bad As It Is

These Things Will Make It Worse

Trying to get the children's bread--, deliverance, without being one of the children can make an already bad situation worse. Praying deliverance type prayers--, decreeing and declaring to demons **that you hang out with** can make it worse. You aren't going to tell these demons anything that they'd obey because you don't have the authority. Go get drunk with your kids and then tell them they have to go to school the next morning because you said so. How far do you think that will go?

Praying and then stopping – turning back from the plow once you have the relief you seek will make things worse – way worse. Praying heavy prayers tonight then tomorrow forming dance covenants with worldly music and lyrics because you now feel *free* – uh oh – not good. It will make things way worse.

Cleanses using demonic potions and the like are not cleanses; they pollute the body even more.

The leaves on the trees are for the healing of the nations. If you do a "spiritual" cleanse and you don't refill with the Spirit of God, the Holy Spirit it is as though your house is swept clean and ready for company. The company is any and every evil demon that can fit in there. Legion had 6000, so there's a lot of room in a human to fill with good or evil. Choose this day, choose every day what you will associate with, let into your life or commune with. You Choose.

Inviting Demons

The takeaway is whatever you're doing is what you are doing. If it is not working for you, then you need to get saved, act saved, sleep saved, and be saved all day when you're awake. If you've invited something evil into your life the ONLY way you will get rid of it is by Jesus Christ. You will not be able to summon up a demon to get rid of another demon. Else the second demon, if stronger, will stay there with you and the torments will be worse than the first, with the lesser demon.

By summoning up, I mean calling a demon up from hell because that is what all these evil witchcraft practices are and that is what they all do. THAT'S NOT **ENERGY** – THAT'S A DEMON, A TALKING THINKING, STRATEGIZING, EVIL DEMON. You will not be able to train it like a dog. It will not sit just because you want it to. You can't even get your kid to behave in public, what are we talking about here? It will schmooze its way into your life, and then **you** will be at *its* mercy if you insist on summoning up demons for revenge, power, fame, money, or for play--, because you just want to see what will happen.

Call a demon, get a demon, get demonized. It's not like you can call up a demon, get what that demon has for you like it's a genie in a bottle and then tell it to go back into the bottle. It doesn't dwell in a bottle; it lives in hell. You unloose it from hell do you think it wants to go back? I mean if we get out of a traffic jam we are not going to want to go back to the jam. People hate inconveniences and demons hate hell, even though that's their ultimate and final address and their time is short. But they will torment and try to draw as many humans as they can with them in the process.

They especially are fond of the ignorant, the rebellious, the sinful and those who don't even know anything about spirits even though they themselves are *spirits*.

Final warning: I'm a good person ain't' gonna cut it. No one can get to the Kingdom of God, no one can get to God except by Jesus Christ. All of us believe we are good people, but we don't get to judge that, the Righteous Judge does.

Jesus is the only Way to get the deliverance that you need and seek.

Epilogue

All this information proves the Word that says, broad is the way to destruction. Narrow is the way to God. If you're doing any of this stuff the first step in deliverance is to STOP! The Bible says, resist the devil, and he will flee from you.

- Get Saved.
- Get Spirit-Filled.
- Pray. Prayers of the righteous avail much power.
- Fast.
- Fast & pray.
- Study. Learn about the problem you're in and how to get out of it and stay out of it!

If you still don't get results, then seek deliverance from a qualified deliverance minister, intercessor, prophet/prophetess, Pastor, or Apostle.

This is not all there is. This is the first email in answer to your question, why is this happening to me?

Grace to you.

Amen.

Christian books by this author:

AK: Adventures of the Agape Kid

AMONG SOME THIEVES

As My Soul Prospers

Behave

Churchzilla (The Wanna-Be Bride of Christ)

The Coco-So-So Correct Show

Demons Hate Questions

Do Not Orphan Your Seed

Do Not Work for Money

Don't Refuse Me Lord

The FAT Demons

got Money?

Let Me Have a Dollar's Worth

Living for the NOW of God

Lord, Help My Debt

Lose My Location

Made Perfect In Love

The Man Safari *(Really, I'm Just Looking)*

Marriage Ed., *Rules of Engagement & Marriage*

The Motherboard: *Key to Soul Prosperity*

My Life As A Slave

Name Your Seed

Plantation Souls

The Poor Attitudes of Money

Power Money: Nine Times the Tithe

The Power of Wealth

Seasons of Grief

Seasons of War

SOULS in Captivity

Soul Prosperity: Your Health & Your Wealth

The *spirit* of Poverty

This Is *NOT* That

The Throne of Grace, *Courtroom Prayers*

Warfare Prayer Against Poverty

When the Devourer is Rebuked

The Wilderness Romance

Other Journals & Devotionals by this author:

The Cool of the Day – Journal *for times spent with God*

got HEALING? Verses for Life

got HOPE? Verses for Life

got WISDOM? Verses for Life

got GRACE? Verses for Life

got JOY? Verses for Life

got PEACE? Verses for Life

got LOVE? Verses for Life

He Hears Us, Prayer Journal *in 4 different colors*

I Have A Star, Dream Journal *in styles for kids, teen, young adult and up.*

I Have A Star, Guided Prayer Journal**, *2 styles*

J'ai une Etoile, Journal des Reves

Let Her Dream, Dream Journal *in multiple colors.*

Men Shall Dream, Dream Journal**, *(blue or black)*

My Favorite Prayers (in 4 styles)

My Sowing Journal (in three different colors)

Tengo una Estrella, Diario de Sueños

Wise Counsel Journal

Illustrated children's books by this author:

Big Dog (8-book series)

Do Not Say That to Me

Every Apple

Fluff the Clouds

I Love You All Over the World

Imma Dance

The Jump Rope

Kiss the Sun

The Masked Man

Not During a Pandemic

Push the Wind

Tangled Taffy

What If?

Wiggle, Wiggle; Giggle, Giggle

Worry About Yourself

You Did Not Say Goodbye to Me

Notes

www.ingramcontent.com/pod-product-compliance
Lightning Source LLC
LaVergne TN
LVHW051420080426
835508LV00022B/3167